# GOSPEL

## HMNS AND SPIRITUALS

# RHYTHM

### FOR PIANO

# & BLUES

## ARRANGED BY BILL WOLAVER

**Moderately Advanced**

*Lillenas* PUBLISHING COMPANY

Kansas City, MO 64141

# CONTENTS

# We're Marching to Zion

ROBERT LOWRY
*Arranged by Bill Wolaver*

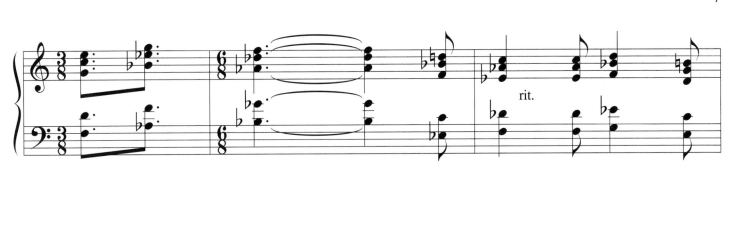

# The Old Rugged Cross

GEORGE BENNARD
*Arranged by Bill Wolaver*

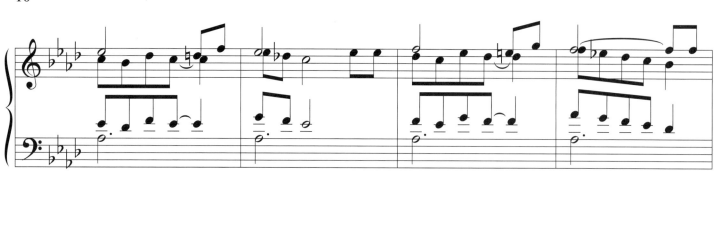

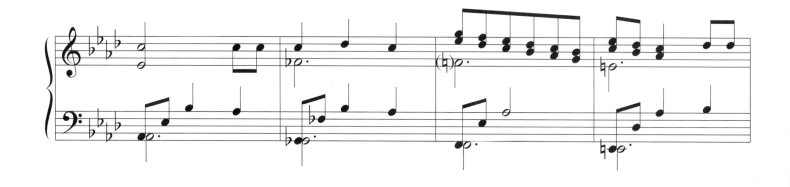

with strength

cresc.

# His Eye Is on the Sparrow

CHARLES H. GABRIEL
*Arranged by Bill Wolaver*

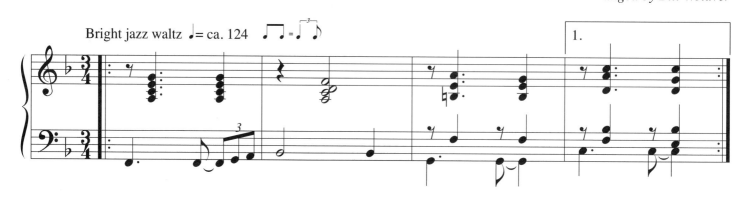

# Deep River

*with*
There Is a Balm in Gilead

Afro-American Spiritual
*Arranged by Bill Wolaver*

With much expression ♩ = ca. 78

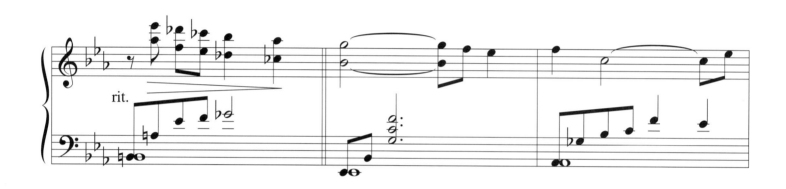

With more movement

"There is a Balm in Gilead"

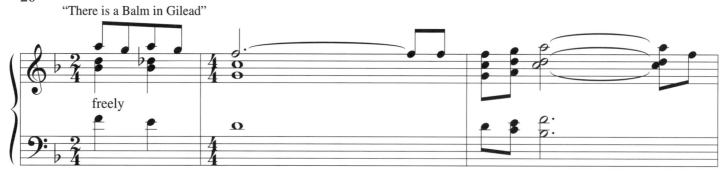

freely

*p*   rit.   cresc.

*f* more expansive

# He Hideth My Soul

WILLIAM J. KIRKPATRICK
*Arranged by Bill Wolaver*

Relaxed ♩ = ca. 82

# Peace in the Midst of the Storm

STEPHEN R. ADAMS
*Arranged by Bill Wolaver*

Restful ♩ = ca. 80

slowing

molto rit.

# When the Saints Go Marching In

Afro-American Spiritual
*Arranged by Bill Wolaver*

# In the Garden

C. AUSTIN MILES
*Arranged by Bill Wolaver*

Gently ♩ = ca. 78

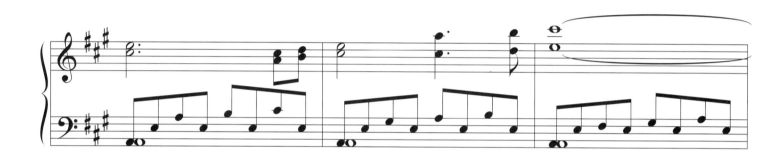

# I'm Bound for the Kingdom

*with*
Goodbye, World Goodbye

MOSIE LISTER
*Arranged by Bill Wolaver*

Moderate blues feel ♩ = ca.88

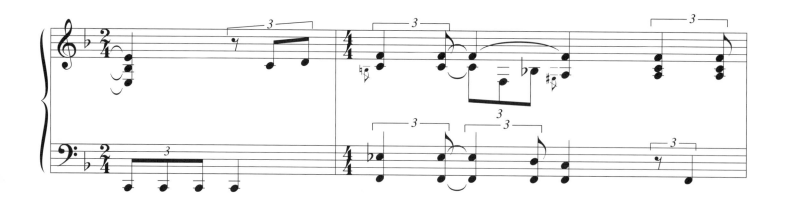

40

Walk that bass!

41

Fast Gospel Feel ♩ = ca. 120

*"Goodbye, World Goodbye"

# What a Friend We Have in Jesus

CHARLES C. CONVERSE
*Arranged by Bill Wolaver*

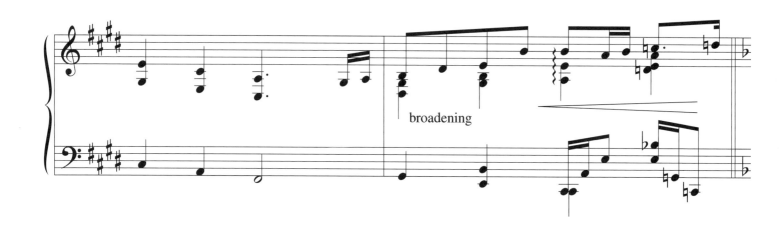